Grow Rich by Reclaiming the American Dream

Al Georges

Grow Rich by Reclaiming the American Dream

Copyright © 2016 by Al Georges

ISBN 13:978-1519766984

Table of Contents

The Vanishing American Dream – Amy and Aspen

Alarm clocks are ringing all across the USA. That's how the new day starts at many homes all across America, and it's no different for Amy and Aspen.

Let's them observe for a while.

For Amy, a single working mom, things are really buzzing. She's rushing to get her daughter, Aspen, out of bed. It's the first day of school and new challenges await both of them.

Aspen, a delightful pixie of a six-year-old, finds many distractions on the way to the kitchen table, where her cereal and milk are waiting for her. She begins to eat her breakfast, ignoring the voices on the television.

Amy is straining to catch some of the day's headlines as the TV anchor broadcasts the financial headlines for the day.

Charles, the anchor, has a warm, authoritative voice. Charles reads the headlines in a staccato bullet fashion, hoping to keep casual viewers tuned in. Charles is not only reading the news, but he also views himself as being affected by what he is reading.

"More than 25 million middle-class families are living paycheck to paycheck, and studies show most have zero savings."

Amy stops in mid-stride. She tilts her head to the side and wonders out loud:

 "Gee, I'm not even middle class. No wonder we run out of money before we run out of month."

AMY TURNS UP THE VOLUME AND BEGINS TO LISTEN INTENTLY.

Charles continues:

"Two-income families, where both parents work to sustain an average lifestyle, have had to overcome the loss of one or both of their jobs and the paychecks that went with them."

"The majority of retired Americans rely solely on Social Security as their only source of income".

The anchor's tone changes, and soon we hear a tease:

"When we come back from commercial, we'll ask our guest financial specialist John an 'intriguing' question. Stay tuned!"

Amy continues to get ready, and the 30-second commercials turn into minutes. Amy keeps a vigilant eye on the clock, not wanting to be late for the first day of school.

Aspen finishes her breakfast, gathers up her school supplies and slowly makes her way to the front door.

Amy stops to listen to the 'intriguing' question before she, too, heads to the door.

Amy is now watching the TV instead of just listening.

The anchor turns to his guest, and asks in an even more authoritative tone:

"John, what would an America with NO Middle class look like?"

John's reply is not totally unexpected by the viewing audience, including Amy.

"Well, what you reported is actually what is happening to many in middle-class America today. A vibrant middle class, which had become a strong point on the landscape of the American economy, is being squeezed. More and more families are sinking into lower-income brackets, but some are also rising from the middle class into the upper middle class.

"You know, Charles, USA Today ran a story in the April 25 2015 Cheat Sheet, under Sam Becker's byline. Its premise is that the U.S. doesn't own the American Dream any more.

"Mr. Becker summarized the article by saying that 'When the American Dream is no longer a realistic goal for most of the American population, it's hard to really say that it remains the land of opportunity.

"He continued by stating "that it is easier to reach the 'American Dream' if you live outside of the United States than it is if you live here."

Amy, with not enough time to do everything she needs to do, shakes her head in disbelief and clicks the remote to the off position.

She shuts the door behind her, but she cannot shut the door on what she's just heard. Amy and Aspen head off to school and work.

Aspen senses her mom has something on her mind, since she's not talking like she usually does when the two of them are going somewhere in the car.

Aspen asks her mother if something is wrong.

"Sorry Aspen," replies Amy. "I was just thinking about my Mom and Dad."

Pulling into a safe area, Amy dials her parent's home.

"Hi Mom. I'm taking Aspen to school, but I was listening to a financial expert on the Channel 2 morning news and I ran out of time to hear all of it."

"You know, we were talking the other day about how you and dad were going through some hard times. I really think you and dad should tune in. Yes, it's on right now on channel 2. But I really need to run. Bye!"

Baby Boomers Home Alone – Bob and Sandra

Sandra, hanging up the phone, calls out to her husband Bob.

Bob, who is 55 years old, and Sandra, who is 53, have both lost their jobs, so they can watch the morning news shows together as they sip their morning coffee.

Bob always teases Sandra that this is their 'Home Alone' moment. Amy, their only daughter, is raising Aspen as a single mom and lives a few blocks away.

"Bob, Amy wanted us to watch the financial expert on Channel 2. He's on right now."

Without hesitation, Bob flips the remote to Channel 2.

The voices coming from the screen are more animated than when Amy had watched. The financial segment has changed from the bullet-point headlines being read earlier to a give-and-take format.

Charles the host is now challenging John the financial expert to provide examples – and to give the audience something to hang onto. Something to take away from this morning's information.

"John, you gave some insight into what's happening to America's middle class and what you described as the 'vanishing American Dream', but you didn't describe what they're feeling."

"Well, Charles, their feelings range from anger and frustration, to depression. One third of American households are classified as living hand to mouth, meaning that they spend all their paychecks.

"Here, at the end of the third quarter, September 2015, the labor participation rate is the lowest it's been in 38 years – an underwhelming 62.6%.

"Charles, over 94 million Americans are no longer in the labor force, and many of these are 'baby boomers' who are being hit hardest with layoffs, job consolidation and outsourcing.

"Then there is what's being called the 'compression of generations' – that's a fancy term to describe the over 25 million adults who live at home with their parents or grandparents because they are unemployed or underemployed.

"Charles, it is not a pretty economic picture."

As John pauses to catch his breath, Charles turns to face the audience at home as the cameras cut away from John. "Stay tuned for our final segment!"

Bob turns the volume down on the commercials so he can ask Sandra about what Amy had said on the phone call.

"Amy just said that she knew we're having a rough time financially since we both lost our jobs. She thought this might shine a light on what options might be out there for us."

Bob shakes his head. "Sandra, you just heard what some experts are saying, but I feel all of it. Frustration and pain at not being able to find a decent job with decent pay. Downsizing, they called it. I'm just too young to retire and my career is over before I am."

Sandra nods silently. She, too, is frustrated and sad at the changes in their lifestyle.

Sandra, eyes glistening, speaks wistfully. "Bob, do you remember when I would take Aspen on a shopping trip and do what grandmothers do best? Just spoil her with attention and little gifts. She always had fun choosing the goodies that we would bring back just for 'grandpa.'"

Those little trips don't come as often; the extra money is just not there anymore.

Bob reaches out and takes Sandra's hand. He gives it a little squeeze, and sighs.

"Sandra, we can make it. I don't know how just yet, but we'll make it through this."

Just then the commercials end, and Charles and John are returned to the viewing audience.

Sandra returns her husband's affectionate squeeze.

"Bob, I know you and I are not the only ones in this same boat. Let's listen."

Financial 'Perfect Storm' – Charles and John

The camera has returned its focus on John, today's financial expert. John has made a career out of appearing as a guest on various network financial programs.

John asks Charles a rhetorical question. "By the way Charles, do you like 'nostalgia questions'? Do you remember the movie, "The Perfect Storm"?

"I bet you do, but for our audience, let me share this brief recap. George Clooney and Mark Wahlberg are two of the main characters in the film. It was made in the year 2000. It's based on an actual weather event that occurred in 1991 and centers on the fishing vessel 'Andrea Gail'.

"It is about the confluence or coming together of two weather systems and the remnants of Hurricane Grace. These three different systems came together in a way that created havoc and destruction, taking 12 lives before it was over.

"Charles, to me, this is what is affecting America's families today. It is a 'perfect storm' that's not only a threat to the American Dream and the vanishing middle class, but a threat to financial security in America."

The camera shifts its focus back to John. Evidently, he's troubled by where this interview is heading.

"John, you're not suggesting that this is a political event, are you?"

John refuses to get into mud-slinging. He smiles, and continues.

"Charles this 'Perfect Storm' is not political or about politics. No matter which side of the political fence we sit on or the size of the boat we're sitting in; financial insecurity affects us all. Whether it's Dad, Mom, our kids, grandparents, friends or relatives. We are all affected. Even future generations will have to pay a price."

Charles poses a follow-up question. "John, can you list what these storm systems are for the benefit of our friends at home?"

"The first financial storm system began forming with the 2007-2008 global financial crisis," he says. "This downturn in economic activity led to the 2008-2012 global recession, from which we still have not recovered. This event has been analyzed before by many others, so I will not take our limited time to replay that history.

"So I'll move on to our second financial storm system. This does not begin at sea, but in our own backyard. This has led to the slowest economic recovery on record for the United States. I'll just read the bullet points and not wander from our main subject.

"They are:

>Massive government spending

>Massive borrowing from China

>Massive amounts of money being printed

>National debt approaching $18 trillion

>Bailouts of banks, institutions and industry while families were left behind to sink or swim on their own

>Over-regulation that stifles economic progress

>Labor participation at its lowest rate

>High-paying jobs being replaced by lower-paying jobs.

Charles turns to John. "I can see how our working families would be affected. Is there more?"

"Yes, Charles, unfortunately there's much more. The third financial storm system looming over the horizon is the retirement dilemma. It affects us in two ways. One way is for those still in the workforce facing what is being called 'the new reality', regarding the vanishing employer-funded retirement plans.

"Many of today's workers no longer have defined-benefit retirement plans available to them. Back in the 1980's, the participation rate in those plans was about 60%. Today, less than 20% of workers have access to defined-benefit retirement plans.

"Making up the shortfall for retirement places an extra burden on working families. How can they make extra income to put into their retirement plan?

"Of course, the second way the retirement dilemma affects us involves those who have already retired. The majority of retired Americans depend solely on Social Security. This is woefully inadequate in meeting any needs beyond basic necessities. So, Charles, people who are unable to continue working in the changing workplace also need to make up the income shortfall. So how do they make extra income to supplement their social security?"

Charles interrupts his guest. "John, you have painted an excellent 'seascape' of the 'Perfect Storm'. You have shown us that not only are Americans in financial trouble, but you have shown that America itself is in trouble."

"Yes, Charles, that leads us to the big conflict today."

The Big Conflict Today –
John's Challenge

Charles summarizes for the viewing audience the points that John has raised so far in today's program. He lists a series of questions he hopes that John will answer before the program ends.

"John, I want you to tie this together for our audience by giving you a list of questions. Ready? Here we go:

"How do we emerge from the Perfect Storm?

"What can Americans do to rebuild Middle Class America?

"Can the American Dream be resurrected?"

"Well, Charles, that's the conflict we face today. It's conflict between 'the rights of personal property' versus the granting of property by the state – the so called re-distribution of wealth.

"President Lyndon Johnson, in his inaugural address in January 1965, called it 'Taking from those who have, to give to those who have not'. Well, that definitely fits the current administration's efforts today. Unfortunately, it amounts to an undeclared 'open border' where millions of immigrants flood past our borders and receive benefits that are designed for American citizens.

"This granting of unappropriated funds by executive order by the Administration further increases the national debt, increases borrowing from China and weakens our anemic economy. The stock market is being underwritten by our federal banking system, which keeps interest rates artificially low.

"Eventually the piper will be paid, but at what cost to America and the tax-paying citizen? Statistics show that approximately only 49 percent of our people actually pay taxes to support the bloated spending currently in place.

Charles interrupts John. "We're running out of time for this segment. Can you summarize what you see as the way for Americans to reclaim the American Dream and find their way to financial freedom?"

John nods in agreement. "What everyone deserves is an opportunity to become all they can be. You know, America was formed and built on what used to be called the Judeo-Christian work ethic and values. Others called it 'rugged individualism'. Today, that model works in America for all religions, races, and nationalities. I think this model would work even better if we stopped being hyphenated Americans.

"Originally, the peoples who reached these shores searching for freedom from persecution began laying a foundation. Their desire for Independence from autocratic rulers led to the War of Independence. It was thought 'noble' during the birthing of America for an individual to become all he could be.

"This coming together of multitudes of individuals, all striving to be all they could be, became the 'force' – a positive 'Perfect Storm' of its own that grew America into the greatest national power in history. This became the power that helped save the world in the First World War. The power that saved the world again from the tyranny of the Axis powers in World War II. The power that turned back the Socialist and Communist movements that enslaved individuals by enslaving whole countries. So, Charles, you and I can both ask, what are America and Americans to do?

"You know, we are once again facing challenges not only from without our borders, but also from within our borders. It is time for 'rugged individualism" to rise again and for all Americans to embrace as 'noble' the quest to become all we can become. John F. Kennedy, our 35th President, said this:

"Let us not seek the Republican answer or the Democratic answer, but the right answer. Let us not seek to fix the blame for the past.

Let us accept our own responsibility for the future."

"Ronald Reagan, our 40th President said this:

"This country was founded and built by people with great dreams and the courage to take great risks."

"John Quincy Adams, our 6th President said this:

"If your actions inspire others to dream more, learn more, do more and become more, you are a leader."

"So, Charles, each of us must answer that call to provide for ourselves and our families. It's not too late to have the American Dream that you and I and count-less others grew up believing in. Each one should strive to become all we can become. Each one of us should help those less fortunate by birth or circum-stance. Each one of us can also become a part of the 'Positive Perfect Storm' that will raise the American Dream and bring our vanishing Middle Class back from the brink of disaster and ruin.

"Let me close with this:

"I believe there are still good and valid opportunities available for those clever enough to take action to re-gain their financial independence and restore the American Dream."

The camera once again focuses on Charles. "John, I want to thank you for presenting a challenge not only to our viewing audience, but to myself too."

"Tune in tomorrow..."

Taking Up the Challenge – Bob and Sandra

Bob and Sandra have not budged from their chairs during the last 30- minute segment of this morning's financial headlines with Charles the host and his special guest, John.

Sandra takes a sip from her cup. "Oh Bob, my coffee's cold. I was so tuned in that I didn't even drink my coffee. How's yours?"

Laughing, Bob says; "Mine is cold, too. I have an idea. Let's make a fresh pot of coffee, turn off the TV and go out to the patio."

Sandra recognizes Bob's signal for an upcoming meaningful discussion. Moving out to the patio had always been where Bob had his serious alone time. Out on the patio, away from the kids, the TV and the phone, Bob was able to laser-focus his thinking.

"O.K., I'm getting the serving tray and the coffee ready. I'll join you in a few minutes. Would you like juice or water with your coffee?"

Bob doesn't answer, as he's already lost in thought and heading through the doorway.

Sandra opts for the water and small snacks to go with their second pot of coffee. Laying the serving tray on the patio table, she looks around for Bob.

"Bob, where are you? "

"Over here, by the fence. I was just looking out at this big world around us. Sometimes we're so focused on our little part of it and forget that we have a place in the big world, not just the little picture."

Sandra asks, "Are you ready for coffee yet?"

Bob shakes his head. "Not yet."

He pauses, and looks at Sandra. "Sandra, what did you like best about what we just heard?"

"Hmmm," Sandra smiles. "I didn't know we were going to have a test. But let me ask you first. What did you like best?"

"Well, Sandra, I actually liked all of it. I'm glad Amy called you.

"It was just what I needed to hear. I've been sitting here, feeling sorry for myself, so angry and frustrated. I forgot who I am, and what I am. I forgot about my strengths and abilities."

Sandra nodded in agreement. "I guess we were going through the anger and denial stages of resentment of both losing our jobs."

"You asked earlier what did I like best. I really liked what John, today's guest said on the program."

"He said, 'There are still good and valid opportunities for those who are clever enough to take action.'"

Bob, turning to Sandra, uses a dancing analogy. "Do you want to lead or follow?"

Both Bob and Sandra realized long ago that it was better for one to lead these discussions and for the other to follow and play Devil's advocate.

Taking turns like this always led to more productive sessions and saved their relationship from bruised egos and hurt feelings.

"I'll lead," says Sandra. "You can concentrate on the pros and cons of what options we consider."

"Fair enough."

Sandra begins the process. "First, Bob you are 55 years old. Do you want a full-time job, or just the income that comes with it?"

Bob quickly agrees that it's not another job he wants, but another income.

"Good. I like having you at home." Sandra continues: "Bob, you're very analytical. How would day trading or the Forex currency exchange appeal to you?"

Bob reminds Sandra that in the last days of August, the markets crashed in reaction to China's devaluation of its currency.

"Sandra, one estimate stated that in the first two days of the crash, $1.4 trillion of value was lost. Not only that, but during the selloff, Mom and Pop and small investors were kept out of the market by what was called a 'technical glitch'. Those investors lost another

2 trillion dollars of value. I think the SEC is investigating what happened, but they cannot restore those investors' money."

Using his comedic voice, he mimics a comedic line he once heard: "Duh, I don't think so, Sandra."

"What about offering customer service from home?" asks Sandra. "You know, a company routes customer calls to our P.C., and you answer questions for their customers."

Bob tosses the question back to Sandra. "Well, I would need to improve my computer skills, learn that company's business and have to be available at the times and days that they set for me. I'll think about it, but I don't see it paying what we need to make."

Sandra scratches her head and is ready to call this session to an end, but she tries one more time.

"Bob, I have a question with two options. How would you feel about either starting our own business or trying a franchise business?"

"Sandra, do you remember when Charlie and his wife tried buying into a franchise? It required a major investment. Charlie said it was more like buying an 80-hour-a-week job, and they still had to do most of the work."

"And now, with the Affordable Care Act, it was just ruled that franchisees are treated as a major employer instead of a 'mom-and-pop' store. I don't think the reward would offset all the costs and regulations."

Both Bob and Sandra feel their frustration level rising. They see that this is not the best way to examine their options.

"Sandra, we've just started our search. I know there's a way to turn our financial fortunes around. Let's see what some of our friends have found out."

The Invitation

Sandra is on the phone with her daughter. "Amy, your dad wanted me to call and say thanks for letting us know about the financial program yesterday. He said it was exactly what he needed to hear. He's determined to find some way for us to get back on our feet. Bob said he would take a job if he could find a decent opportunity. You know how hard it is to get an offer when you're 55."

Amy nods in agreement, "Mom, believe me, it's also hard for me to find a decent opportunity – and I have a college degree I have to pay for!"

Amy changes the conversation. "By the way, do you remember Mr. and Mrs. Bennett?"

Sandra tries to recall the couple. "Oh, do you mean the couple who taught you in Sunday school?"

"That's them." Amy is excited that her mom remembered them. "I ran into Mary Bennett at the gas station on the way home tonight. She asked about you and dad."

Sandra, almost ashamed about not having a job, is always guarded when she runs into someone who knows her and Bob.

"Amy, what did you say?"

"I said you and dad were both doing fine, but like a lot of people, you were both trying to find new jobs."

Sandra doesn't appreciate Amy's candor with others. "Amy, I hate letting people know our situation."

"Mom, it's okay. As a matter of fact, Mary told me that, now that they have no jobs, they earn even more income than when they did."

Sandra is surprised. "Really? They earn more income than when they were working? How'd they do that?

"Really, Mom. Mary thought maybe we would visit them to learn what they're doing to earn income."

Thinking it over, Sandra decides to talk to Bob about meeting with the Bennett's.

Soon, Bob arrives at the front door.

"Honey, I'm home!" This is Bob's light-hearted ritual.

"Sandra, where are you?"

Her voice floats through the open window. "Out here on the patio. I have some fresh lemonade and cookies fresh out of the oven."

Bob pauses, puts the mail on the table, and muses out loud … "Hmmm, the patio, lemonade and cookies. We must be fixin' to have a discussion."

Bob walks out to the patio. "That lemonade sure looks good. What's the occasion?"

"Honey, honestly, I am not trying to soften you up, but do you remember Amy's Sunday school teachers? The ones she had when she was in fifth grade?"

Bob, sipping his lemonade, reaches for a cookie with his free hand. "Yes, I remember them. I liked Ted. He's what you would call one of the good guys. Why, do you ask?"

Sandra tells about Amy meeting Mary Bennett earlier that day.

"Amy and Mary saw each other when they were filling up their cars at the gas station. It was funny, the two of them meeting that way after not having seeing each other for so long. Mary asked Amy about us and how we were doing. Amy told her we were without jobs and trying to start new careers.

"Amy said that Ted and Mary have found something that lets them make money without having to hold steady jobs. Bob, I'm kind of curious. Why don't we visit with them?"

Bob knows that resistance is futile. He takes the last bite of his cookie. Lemonade and cookies out on the patio: Sandra left him with no way out of this.

"Do we still have that church directory with their phone number? I'll give Ted a call."

Soon, Bob returns to the patio. "We're set up for to-morrow night. They wanted us to come to a business meeting tonight, but I told them we wanted a private meeting."

Home Visit and Interview with Mary and Ted

Sitting outside around the usual gathering spot, Sandra has set a dessert tray along with a fresh pot of coffee and a pitcher of iced tea on the patio table.

Ted and Mary have just arrived and have quickly been welcomed as longtime friends, although it has been several years since they've seen each other. Sandra reminisces about the days when the four of them were members of the same church and shared many fellowship meals.

Bob observes that a lot has happened since those days. He pokes fun at the extra pounds and thinning hair he now wears.

Ted agrees. "I think you're right, Bob. We all feel that way when the possibilities in our lives seem endless."

Sandra, not wanting to omit the women's point of view, which is usually more practical than her husband's, pipes up. "Then life happens. Reality happens. We end up changing our plans to care for the daily challenges we're faced with. We end up not doing what we planned, but doing the best we can."

Bob, wanting to get to the reason for getting together, offers dessert and coffee to their guests.

Ted, having made these home presentations many times before, knows that Bob and Sandra are ready to hear his message.

"Bob, I want you to know that Mary and I had planned to call on you and Sandra about our business venture, but we've been busy helping others to start their own. So we're glad you called and invited us to come over."

Sandra turns to Mary. "I was curious about what Amy said you and Ted were doing. Our new reality is that we're both in our 50s and we've both lost our jobs. Frankly, we wanted to look at different options to turn our finances around."

Ted leans forward. "Sandra, let me share what Mary and I have learned. Bob, how about you? What method of research works best for you?"

Bob, thinking to himself, doesn't want to sound too eager or receptive. "Well, I used to conduct interviews for our college newspaper. How about I interview you and Mary?"

Ted smiles, grabs a cookie and nods his approval.

Bob returns to the patio where Ted, Mary and Sandra are waiting for him to return with his notepad. Bob is about to interview Ted and Mary about their business venture.

Bob: Ted, how would you describe the business you're in?

Ted: Mary and I are involved in a 'Home-Based Business'.

It lets us develop our own personal distributor base by representing some exciting proprietary products in the Nutritional Health and Wellness marketplace.

Bob: Whoa!

Ted, can you say that again in simple language?

Ted: Sure. In simple terms, we, share information with other people who might benefit or have an interest in the amazing products we represent.

Our business is based on meeting the demand for natural, health-enhancing products from people who want to be pro-active in maximizing their health.

Bob: Well, Sandra and I are both know that not only people in our age group, but nearly all ages are more health-conscious now than they were 10 or 20 years ago.

Ted: Exactly. Let me lay it on the line, Bob. There's money to be made here. Just how much depends on the value of our service to others. Here's what I mean.

When I was about 10 years old, my mother took me to see a doctor whose office was in a tall building. The elevators in those days required a full-time attendant to take people up and down the many floors. I was amazed that one man would ride up and down, hundreds of times per day, taking people to the right floor.

Bob, let me ask you, who do you think earned more money each day? The doctor who healed the sick, or the man who went up and down all day long? They both had honorable jobs, but which one provided the most value, the most service?

Bob: I would have to say the doctor, Right?

Ted: Exactly. Bob, which is why we share the business side of the opportunity that these products offer people just like Sandra and you. You already know that many people are suffering in today's economy.

The reality is layoffs, downsizing, low pay, no true career path, no retirement plans, no savings. Record numbers of people are no longer looking for a job. Too many have given up on the American dream.

We have a system and method in place to help those who want to take control of their lives by gaining their financial freedom.

Bob: You know, I heard a man once say that "you can have anything in life you want, if you just help enough other people get what they want."

Ted, are there enough other people out there looking for what you have?

Ted: Bob, I actually met the man who said that. I attended one of his seminars in Dallas and heard Ol' Zig Zigglar say that in person. I still cherish the autograph and hearty handshake I received that day.

The simple answer to your question is yes. Multitudes of people not only need our products, but are actively looking for ways to improve their health and their finances.

Both you and Sandra fit into the category of people who are wondering about the money-making potential of their own business.

So we're tapping into two different segments of society.

They are the health-conscious market, and the business-opportunity segment.

Bob: "Ted, this is not a Pyramid scheme or scam, is it?"

Ted: "No Bob, but I am glad you asked that up front. Many people have bought into the urban legend that networking is a pyramid scam.

"Marketing through a Home-Based Distributor Network is a legitimate and legal business model. It allows for the mass distribution of products without having to go through wholesalers, distribution brokers, agents and other middlemen normally found in retail distribution of products."

Look at it this way. What this means to you and Sandra and our team of independent distributors is that the savings to our company in distribution costs, advertising budgets, administration and labor costs are passed on to our network distributors in the form of substantial compensation.

Bob: I'm new to this concept. Is this something new?

Ted: No. Mary and I did some research, and found that about a thousand companies in America use the network form of distribution.

We even found that several companies began doing business in the 19th century. Lindt Chocolates R.S.V.P began in 1845 and Avon Skincare began in 1886.

Bob: Wow! Anyone else whose names we might recognize?

Ted: Well, Donald Trump wrote the book "Why We Want You to Be Rich" and in it said that, "Network Marketing has proven to be a viable and rewarding source of income".

Warren Buffet's companies include a well-known network marketing company specializing in kitchen items.

Robert Kiyosaki who wrote the "Rich Dad Poor Dad" series of books and was quoted in Prosperity and Success newspaper.

He said: "By its very nature and design, network marketing is a strikingly fair, democratic, socially responsible system of generating wealth."

Bob: I'm impressed, Ted. I think we're ready to hear some specifics about your company.

When I used to submit my interviews to my editor, we would type the number 30 across the bottom of the last page to signify 'the end'.

Ted, this interview is over.

-30-

"Great, Bob," says Ted. "It sounds like you and Sandra are ready to take action and move on to the next step. Am I correct?"

Bob looks over at Sandra and each nods in agreement.

Conclusion On Your Marks, Ready, Set, GO!

Dear Reader,

You have just had an inside look at the many challenging factors that affect today's families.

The factors listed in part 1 of this book are not complete. The missing part is "you". Where "you" find yourself as you read this book becomes a part of the whole story that only you can write.

If you were ever ran track or competed a similar event in your younger days at school, the starter would prepare the competitors in that particular event by declaring: "On your marks, get ready, get set..." and then pull the trigger on the starting pistol.

This was designed to ensure that each competitor had a fair start.

We want you to have a fair start and a fair chance at succeeding.

We want you to truly live a life without limits and to reach the highest levels of success as you define success.

Some of the advantages of owning your own home-based business through the system are:

1) Low initial start-up costs: You choose the beginning level that meets your income or earning expectations.

2) You can choose a time commitment that fits your current schedule. Begin your part-time career opportunity by building upon each level of success.

3) Tax benefits can reduce your overall tax burden.

4) You can instantly plug into an existing successful model without having to develop a product or a marketing program.

5) Your residual income grows as you grow your business. You don't have to be a J. K. Rowling or an Elvis or a Frank Sinatra to build month after month income from your previous efforts.

6) You receive mentoring by the leaders in our company.

7) You get your own replicated website, part of which describes your personal success story.

8) A smartphone application that lets you conduct your business where ever you are.

9) Continuous training through our Online University, corporate and sponsor training calls, and regional and corporate training events.

10) Our Secret Weapon, which will let you build "exponentially" without incurring additional costs. This alone will take you from a "mom-and-pop" business to a national or international presence. Unfortunately,

this proprietary information is reserved for those who take the following action steps.

Action step # 1 – Join the person who referred you to this book, or go to **www.WorkForYourselfNot-ByYourself.com** or **www.AlGeorgesFinancial-Freedom.com** for more details.

Fill in your personal contact information to receive your free, no-obligation, personalized business review.

Action step # 2— Review the Personal Success Journal found in Part 2. This is your private information, for your personal use, and will not be asked of you.

Personal Success Journal

Part 2

Status Quo, or Gung Ho?

"A journey of a thousand miles begins with a single step."

Laozi – Philosopher of Ancient China

Author's note:

Thank you for staying with us to this point in the book.

We really enjoyed bringing Amy, Aspen, Bob, Sandra, Charles, John, Ted, and Alice to you as we shared what is happening in many homes not only in the USA, but across many countries in the world.

We choose not to introduce any particular company in this book, as many reputable networking companies provide products and services designed to improve the lives of those who use their products and services.

The dreams and aspirations are not limited to what we call "The American Dream" in this book.

Rather, it is common to all peoples around the world, as everyone wants to improve their quality of life for themselves and their loved ones.

However, achieving this dream is not common to all individuals.

Rather it is rare, because achieving your dreams is reserved to those who pursue it without limits.

The Personal Success Journal found in Part 2 is designed to guide you in your journey. It is designed to be a brief and easy map to use.

Good Luck

Status Quo? Or Gung Ho!

"For things to change for you, you have to change"

Jim Rohn

How strong is your personal desire to change your financial destiny?

1	2	3	4	5	6	7
8	9	10				

On a scale from 1 to 10 (1 equals weak desire; 10 is strong desire)

Rate where you see yourself on this scale.

Hint: if you circled 4 or less, Stop here! Don't go any further! Your journey is over.

Your sponsor and mentor would only be able to do this for you if your desire is strong enough to complete the journey.

If you circled from 5 to 7, take time to see what it would take for you to elevate to an 8 to 10 rating.

Below, list the specific changes or improvements you want to realize on this journey.

Income
_____

Career
_____

Home
_____

Lifestyle
_____

Other #1
_____

Other #2
_____

The Power of Choice

"We live not as we wish to, but as we can."

Menander, Greek Author circa 342 BC

"The mass of men (and women) lead lives of quiet desperation, and go to the grave with the song still in them."

Henry David Thoreau

As you can see from the quotations above, most of us don't get to live our wishes. We lead lives dictated by circumstance.

Thoreau reflected that the majority of us lead lives of quiet desperation. Today's news headlines would question how quiet that desperation is.

Studies have shown that just a few extra hundred dollars per month would make a big difference in the lives of many families.

Human Potential Teacher Brian Tracy puts it this way:

"I found every single successful person I've ever spoken to had a turning point. The turning point was when they made a clear, specific, unequivocal decision that they were going to achieve success. Some people make that decision at 15, some people make it at 50, and most people never make it at all."

So, is this your turning point?

Have you made that clear, specific, unequivocal decision to be successful?

List your turning point on the line below. No one else will see this.

_____

Now list some daily action points that will keep you on the correct heading.

(Examples: Cutting back on watching TV, setting a definite daily start time, setting activity goals)

_____

_____

_____

_____

Training Camp

A) Being Coachable

B) Your Why

C) Commitment

The whistle around the coach's neck is not only a shrill call to stop the play. It's also a symbol of authority. He or she is the person in charge, the person responsible for setting the team's course and the individual player's actions.

As a Pop Warner coach for my kid's taxi squad, I found the boys were too small or inexperienced to play in the competitive league, so they gained experience learning the basics by playing other taxi-squad teams.

This was not my first excursion in leading others to team and individual goals.

I served as a training school manager for a fast-food chain and as Training Director for a multi-state division of the same national chain.

Whether it was coaching 8-year-old boys or training grown men in the operation of a million-dollar food operation, the reward consisted of seeing the light in their eyes when they grasped the concepts of making a perfect block or hitting the profit-and-loss goals for their restaurant.

I will not be there in person to see the light bulb turn on when you grasp the lesson or when you take action to turn your dreams into reality.

The reward and validation of the coach and mentor lays in the success of the individuals he or she is training.

Dr. Bob Butera wrote: "When the Student is ready, the Teacher appears."

I hope that you and I are both ready.

So, are you coachable?

In this industry, we're fond of saying; "You are in business for yourself, but not by yourself." Meaning that you will be assisted and guided in your business venture by your sponsor or mentor. The value of this personal guidance depends on both the quality and efforts of your sponsor trainer and on your own efforts.

Your efforts will lead to success or failure.

If I were to ask others of you, would they say you are 'coachable'? _____

Would they say you are 'trainable'?

_____

I feel being trainable and coachable are two different things. One takes place in practice, and the other while you are playing the game.

Would they say you play well with others?

_____

Success in this business is enhanced when you can build your own team, where you are compensated for helping others do what you are doing.

Do you see yourself as a 'leader'?

_____

Are you willing to work on improving yourself?
_____

We find that self-improvement magnifies your earning potential.

This opportunity is truly without financial limits.

I encourage you to get with the person who gave you a copy of this book.

Or go to one of my sites:

www.AlGeorgesFinancialFreedom.com

or

www.WorkForYourselfNotByYourself.com for more details.

Working on your "Why"

One of the 'key' puzzle pieces to your success will be your ability to articulate exactly why you invested in your own home-based business.

If you have a "bricks-and-mortar" operation where people come to you for your service or product, the customer accepts your 'why' without it being stated.

My personal 'why' revolves around several anchor points.

The first is the personal health benefits I gained by taking the product. It truly changed my life. The second is the personal health benefits that my friends and customers gain by using the product.

The third is my personal mission. My business is a force for good that nurtures and safeguards the health and prosperity of all to whom God leads me to serve.

But enough about me. I listed the above as an example of what a "why" looks like.

A healthy dissatisfaction with how things are going for you might form a part of your why. Overcoming limits to your lifestyle or income limits due to conditions beyond your control can also become part of your why.

My mentors stress the importance of my personal 'why' being strong enough to enable me to power through the hard times and obstacles that come with every opportunity.

Please describe your personal why

_____

_____

_____

Please describe a financial why

_____

_____

Optional – describe a humanitarian why

_____

_____

Commitment

One of my many favorite writers, Og Mandino, wrote the following:

"The Opportunity has been wasted unless I have the guts, the persistence, and the willpower to follow the plan through to its fruition."

Our company and your sponsor/trainer have a plan of action that has been successful for their independent distributors.

Being in business for yourself lets you make all the decisions about how you'll market your business.

You can choose how much guidance you want or need. Ideally, your sponsor will want to continue to expand his business by helping others in addition to helping you.

By the same token, building your network of affiliated distributors is similar to franchising yourself with an ever-increasing level of sales and income.

Please write your personal commitment statement that will guide your daily, weekly and monthly action and activity plans.

_____

_____

_____

Be sure to make a strong and irrevocable commitment to give all that you have and to give all that you are to achieve your vision, goals and lifestyle.

_____

_____

_____

Final Thoughts

We just took a walk down any street, in any town U.S.A; and we glimpsed into the soul of many family scenes playing out across this once prosperous nation.

One of my favorite philosophers, Jim Rohn left us a legacy of wisdom to draw upon before he left this world. His audio series: "Take Charge of your Life"; contains a section devoted to the struggles many are facing today.

Mr. Rohn states in this audio series that the answers we are searching for can be readily found if one searches. Just thinking of his wisdom on this, I can hear his golden voice and manner and inflection re-sounding in my mind.

Rohn laments that what they were searching was there for them but: **"They missed the book."**

Masterfully he repeats; "They missed the book; They didn't read the book."

Thank you so much for reading this book.

Hopefully you will take the next step in pursuing your financial destiny however you define your destiny.

Visit my site: www.AlGeorgesFinancialFreedom.com and leave a message.